Night's Quiet B

Stars like jewels softly gleam,
In a sky that's vast and dream.
Moonlight spills like silver wine,
Wrapping earth in sleep divine.

Whispers carried by the breeze,
Rustling through the ancient trees.
Crickets serenade the night,
In this calm, all feels just right.

Blankets made of velvet dark,
Hide the world from every spark.
Dreams take flight on whispers' wings,
Underneath what quiet brings.

Stillness holds the moment dear,
Every heartbeat, crystal clear.
Nature's lullaby unfolds,
As the night with wonder molds.

In this hush, we drift away,
Lost in thoughts that swirl and sway.
Night's embrace, so sweet and wide,
In its quiet, we'll abide.

The Solitude of a Snowy Evening

Snowflakes descend in silence fair,
Blanketing the world with care.
Footprints lost in white expanse,
A tranquil, frozen, delicate dance.

Windows glow with warmth inside,
While outside, shadows gently bide.
In the solitude, I find peace,
As the chaos of life does cease.

Pines adorned in coats of white,
Sway softly in the moon's soft light.
Whispers carried on the chill,
Invite reflection, still and ill.

A cup of tea warms the hand,
As snowflakes twirl and softly land.
In this moment, time stands still,
Embracing the night, a heart to fill.

The solitude wraps me tight,
In its grasp, everything feels right.
Underneath a snowy shroud,
I find solace, sweet and proud.

Weaving Tales in the Frosty Air

Breathe out whispers in the night,
Frosty air glistens with light.
Each exhale a tale to share,
In the chill hangs magic rare.

Scarves pulled tight around our necks,
We venture forth, no need for flecks.
Stories woven with each step,
As the world around us wept.

Moonbeams kiss the frosted ground,
In the hush, the quiet sound.
Echoes of our laughter blend,
With the snowflakes as they descend.

Fingers brush against the frost,
In this moment, never lost.
We weave the threads of who we are,
Underneath this twinkling star.

With each breath, the tales we spin,
In the cold, we feel the kin.
Frosty memories fill the air,
Weaving magic everywhere.

Frozen Whispers in the Night

The snowflakes fall with grace,
Each one a silent dream,
They dance upon the air,
In stillness, they redeem.

Beneath the hush of stars,
The world is wrapped in white,
A blanket soft and warm,
A tranquil, frozen night.

The trees wear coats of frost,
Their branches gently sway,
While shadows slip and slide,
Through the night, they play.

A whisper through the pines,
A secret, soft and near,
The winter calls to me,
In silence, I can hear.

In every breath I take,
The chill kisses my skin,
A moment held in time,
Where dreams begin to spin.

Silent Dance of Winter's Veil

The frost adorns the ground,
In patterns lace and fine,
Each step a quiet sound,
As shadows intertwine.

Underneath the moon's glow,
The world begins to close,
Wrapped in winter's embrace,
The silence gently flows.

The stars, they twinkle bright,
Like diamonds in the sky,
Each one a whispered wish,
A night's soft lullaby.

The air is crisp and clear,
With magic in its breath,
While nature spins her tale,
Of life and quiet death.

In twilight's soft caress,
Time lingers, breathless, still,
As winter's dance unfolds,
With grace and endless thrill.

Moonlight on Crystal Blankets

The moonlight spills like cream,
Across the fields so wide,
Where shadows weave and wane,
In the winter's stride.

Each crystal flake that falls,
Reflects the silver beams,
A canvas pure and bright,
Where nature softly dreams.

The night is calm and vast,
A whisper to the night,
With every breath I take,
I feel the world's delight.

Beneath this tranquil sky,
The silence wraps around,
A blanket thick with stars,
Where peace and hope abound.

With every step I make,
The crunch, a song of snow,
Woven through the silence,
In winter's gentle glow.

Ethereal Dreams in Silver Drift

The dreams within the snow,
Are secrets left untold,
Whispers of the night,
In starlit hues of gold.

Each flake is born anew,
A story in the air,
As winter weaves her magic,
With utmost tender care.

Beneath the sky's embrace,
The earth holds its soft breath,
While silvery moonlight
Falls gently, life and death.

These moments feel so vast,
In stillness, peace resides,
As dreams drift on the breeze,
Through time and endless tides.

In every fleeting thought,
A world of wonder spun,
These ethereal dreams,
In silver drift, we run.

The Softest Touch of Winter's Kiss

In the hush of night, a shimmer falls,
A blanket of white, soft as whispers.
Trees don their gowns of icy lace,
As dreams entwine in winter's embrace.

The air is crisp, each breath a cloud,
Footsteps muffled, the world feels proud.
Shadows dance beneath the pale moon,
A serenade of frost, a gentle tune.

Children's laughter breaks the still,
Snowflakes swirling, a magical thrill.
Snowmen rise with a cheerful grin,
As winter's spell begins to spin.

Warmth inside, as cold winds blow,
Fire crackles, casting a glow.
Cocoa sipped by the twilight's gleam,
In the softest touch, life feels like a dream.

Embrace the chill, let spirits soar,
In winter's arms, we yearn for more.
The season's whispers, sweet and light,
In its gentle hold, we find delight.

Secrets of the Night Unfurled in Snow

Beneath the stars, the silence breathes,
A tapestry sewn with silver leaves.
Whispers of night, so soft and low,
Reveal the secrets wrapped in snow.

With every flake, a story spun,
Of lost moments beneath the sun.
The cool air hums a hidden tune,
Tales of shadows, magic's boon.

Each step taken leaves a mark,
In the cold embrace, light meets dark.
The world transforms, a dreamlike sight,
As secrets bloom in the soft, white night.

Glimmers glitter on branches bare,
A crisp stillness hangs in the air.
Nature's palette, painted slow,
As darkness cradles the ancient snow.

In the midst of whispers, spirits glide,
Night's soft secrets we cannot hide.
Drifting softly, they intertwine,
In the snowy silence, hearts align.

Stars Adrift in the Silent Drift

In cosmic grace, the stars descend,
A gentle drift around the bend.
The night unfolds, a velvet sheet,
Where dreams and stardust softly meet.

With quiet glows, the heavens shine,
Unfurling tales of the divine.
Wishes whispered, freely cast,
In the silent drift, the die is cast.

Galaxies spun in swirling dance,
Inviting us to join the trance.
Celestial bodies weave and roam,
In the cosmos, we find our home.

Awash in wonder, lost in time,
Each heartbeat echoes a soft chime.
Stars above, like lanterns bright,
Guide the soul through the endless night.

Embrace the magic, feel it rise,
As stars adrift light up the skies.
In this cosmic cradle, we reside,
With hearts wide open, let love guide.

Flakes that Whisper Forgotten Tales

Falling softly, the flakes cascade,
A quilt of silence, a serenade.
Each flake a whisper, a tale retold,
Of forgotten dreams in the winter cold.

They dance and twirl, so light and free,
Silent echoes of what used to be.
Memories wrapped in frost's embrace,
In every flake, a fleeting trace.

The world holds its breath in wonder's gaze,
As winter weaves through nature's maze.
Among the branches, stories bind,
In the frozen air, warmth defined.

As twilight whispers secrets near,
The flakes unite, the past is clear.
In their gentle fall, we find our peace,
In winter's hand, our worries cease.

So let the snowflakes tell their tale,
In every drift, our hopes prevail.
For in each flake, life's dance remains,
Whispering sweetly of heart's refrains.

Frosted Echoes in a Distant Land

In silent woods where shadows creep,
The frosted air begins to weep.
Echoes dance on crystalline skies,
While winter's breath softly sighs.

Branches lace with icy sheen,
Nature's beauty, calm and serene.
Footsteps mark the path of dreams,
Whispers ride on silver beams.

A distant call from lands unknown,
In every flake, a story's sewn.
Through frost-kissed fields and mountains grand,
Awake the heart in this vast land.

Stars above twinkle like souls,
In this tranquil world, time unrolls.
Frosted echoes, memories spun,
In a land where shadows run.

So let us wander, hand in hand,
Through swirling snow, across the sand.
With dreams as vast as open seas,
In frosted echoes, we find peace.

Polished Dreams in Glittering White

Beneath the moon, a field so wide,
Where polished dreams and hopes reside.
Each flake that falls, a sparkling tale,
In the night, they softly sail.

Icicles hang like crystal spears,
Reflecting stories of our fears.
Yet in the glow of shimmering light,
We find our courage, pure and bright.

A gentle breeze whispers along,
Guiding the lost with a sweet song.
In glittering white, all seems anew,
With every heartbeat, a promise true.

As dawn awakens the sleepy night,
Our polished dreams take graceful flight.
Bathed in warmth of the rising sun,
A world reborn, the day has begun.

So let us chase what dreams inspire,
Through winter's chill, hearts blaze like fire.
In this embrace of snow and light,
We find our strength, our future bright.

Whispers of the Frosted Night

In the hush of a frosted night,
Whispers roam in gentle flight.
Stars above, a silent choir,
Each twinkle fuels our heart's desire.

Moonlight casts a ghostly veil,
As shadows weave a secret tale.
Through icy breath and chilling air,
A promise lingers, calm and rare.

Footsteps crunch on frosted ground,
In every sound, magic is found.
Wrapped in dreams both soft and bright,
We wander through the quiet night.

Nature sings in muted tones,
A lullaby that soothes our bones.
Whispers of hope float on the breeze,
In frosty moments, hearts find ease.

So let us treasure every sigh,
For in this cold, our spirits fly.
Embrace the night, let worries fade,
In whispers soft, our lives are made.

When the World Holds Its Breath

Soft whispers dance in the air,
Nature pauses, a moment rare.
The sky painted in muted hues,
As day ends, the night ensues.

Shadows stretch, then softly creep,
Crickets sing their lullabies deep.
Stars awaken, twinkling bright,
In the hush of gathering night.

A heartbeat felt beneath the stars,
The world sighs with its hidden scars.
Time stands still, a sacred space,
Where silence holds a gentle grace.

The moon rises, a watchful eye,
Lighting paths for dreams to fly.
In this moment, peace is found,
As the earth spins, soft and profound.

When the world holds its breath so tight,
Each soul basks in the quiet light.
Together we linger, hearts entwined,
In this magic, our souls aligned.

Enchanted Silence of the Twilight Hours

In the twilight, shadows blend,
Golden hues begin to mend.
Whispers of the fading day,
As the sun drifts away.

Stars peek through the dusky veil,
A soft breeze tells a tale.
Chirping crickets, a gentle band,
Nature's music, perfectly planned.

Moonlit paths begin to glow,
In the magic, time moves slow.
A symphony of fading light,
Wrapped in the arms of night.

Dreams unfold in soft embrace,
Lost in this enchanting space.
Every heartbeat falls in line,
With the rhythm, all divine.

In this moment, magic dwells,
Where silence weaves its soothing spells.
Twilight whispers, secrets shared,
In the stillness, souls are bared.

Glimmering Ghosts of the Past

In the corridors of the mind,
Memories linger, intertwined.
Echoes of laughter, shadows cast,
Living in glimmering ghosts of the past.

Photographs fade, yet the smiles stay,
Time can't take those dreams away.
Fleeting moments, crystal clear,
Haunting whispers that we hold dear.

Voices calling from afar,
Guiding us like a distant star.
In dreams they dance, so alive,
In the heart, they still survive.

Weaving tales of joy and sorrow,
In every dusk, there's a tomorrow.
Lessons learned, each stitch a thread,
In the tapestry of what's been said.

Embrace the past, let it flow,
For in its grace, we truly grow.
Glimmering ghosts forever near,
In our hearts, we'll keep them here.

Frosted Serenade in the Stillness

Winter wraps the world in white,
Blanketing earth, pure and bright.
Snowflakes dance in the chilly air,
Whispering secrets everywhere.

Trees stand tall, adorned in frost,
Nature sleeps, a paradise lost.
Each breath a cloud, a ghostly plume,
In the silence, we find our room.

Footsteps crunch on the snowy ground,
In solitude, a peace is found.
Cold winds carry a silent song,
In winter's grasp, we all belong.

Twinkling stars in the endless night,
Kindling hearts with their gentle light.
In this frosted serenade,
We find the solace winter made.

So let us pause, embrace the chill,
In the stillness, we find our will.
Wrapped in warmth, though cold it seems,
Winter's magic sings through dreams.

Shivering Shadows of Solitude

In the silence, whispers creep,
Beneath the trees, secrets seep.
Moonlight dances on the ground,
In the stillness, shadows are found.

Echos of laughter fade away,
Crisp leaves tell tales of yesterday.
Lonely stars twinkle above,
A haunting serenade of love.

The night holds a cold embrace,
Each breath fades, a fleeting trace.
With every heartbeat, I recede,
In solitude's clutch, I plant the seed.

Whispers form in the stark air,
Fleeting moments, light as a prayer.
Fog drapes over the weary ground,
In this stillness, peace is found.

Murmurs of dreams softly swell,
In the shadows, I weave my spell.
Lonely paths I wander deep,
In solitude, the secrets keep.

Surrendering to the Winter's Breath

Silent flakes begin to fall,
Covering the world, a white shawl.
Chill winds whisper through the night,
Nature's peace, pure and bright.

The trees stand tall, adorned in white,
Each branch a story, a silent plight.
Footsteps crunch beneath my feet,
In this realm where cold and warm meet.

Frosted windows, a cozy glow,
Inside, the warmth begins to flow.
With every sip, I feel the cheer,
Surrendering to winter, drawing near.

In the distance, a river glows,
Reflecting light as the cold wind blows.
Nature wraps us, a muted song,
In the winter's breath, we belong.

Beneath the stars, the world is still,
In the quiet, the heart does fill.
With every breath, I feel alive,
In winter's arms, I gladly thrive.

Lost in the Quiet

Whispers of the evening air,
Softly beckon, calm and rare.
Every sound gently fades away,
In the stillness, I long to stay.

Moonlit paths and shadowed trees,
A tranquil heart finds its ease.
Burdened thoughts begin to drift,
In silence, my spirit lifts.

Stars emerge in velvet night,
Each one a wish, a guiding light.
Lost in dreams, I float above,
In the quiet, I feel love.

The world outside ceases to be,
Within this calm, I am free.
Every heartbeat, a gentle hum,
In the quiet, I find my drum.

Dusk embraces the weary day,
In starlit skies, I find my way.
Wrapped in silence, I find the key,
To the depths of this mystery.

The Artistry of a Quiet Evening

Brushstroke skies bleed into night,
Sunset fades with its soft light.
Colors dance, a gentle stir,
In stillness, the world does confer.

Shadows fall with grace and care,
Painting landscapes, pure and rare.
As twilight hums a soothing tune,
I savor the magic of the moon.

In the hush, time seems to sway,
Golden moments drift away.
Every whisper, a treasured sound,
In this quiet, life is profound.

Stars emerge, a gallery bright,
Each twinkle tells a story's light.
In the calm, orange blush departs,
Creating art within our hearts.

The evening breathes, a canvas wide,
Each moment weaves, the day is tied.
Colors soften, shadows blend,
In the quiet, I find my friend.

Elysium Draped in Diamond Dust

Beneath the stars so bright, we tread,
In fields where dreams and wishes spread.
The night adorned in shining light,
Whispers secrets of pure delight.

Around us sparkles gently play,
Each moment drifts like soft ballet.
In silence, hearts begin to sing,
A symphony of hope we bring.

Glowing paths of silver trace,
In Elysium, we find our grace.
With every breath, the magic flows,
As diamond dust around us glows.

Embracing all the dreams we chase,
In this ethereal, timeless space.
Together we shall weave the night,
In an embrace of purest light.

A tapestry of stars unfurl,
In diamond dust, our spirits whirl.
Through every shadow, hope will bloom,
As love ignites the endless room.

A Night of Crystal Dreams Unfolded

Amidst the glow of twilight's hue,
A longing heart finds peace anew.
In whispers soft as silken breeze,
A world of dreams beneath the trees.

The moon, a lantern in the sky,
Reflects the hopes that never die.
With every note of night's sweet song,
Our souls entwine, where we belong.

Beneath the stars, the magic swells,
In crystal dreams that time compels.
We dance upon the dewy grass,
As shadows of our worries pass.

The air is filled with sweet perfume,
As nature weaves its gentle loom.
In every heartbeat, freedom calls,
Where silence deepens, love enthralls.

In moments lost to fleeting time,
We rise as one, in spirit, rhyme.
A night adorned in dreams untold,
In crystal whispers, hearts unfold.

Harmonies of Ice in Enchanted Stillness

In winter's grasp, the world is hush,
A frozen realm where hearts can rush.
Beneath the moon's soft silver glow,
Harmonies of ice begin to flow.

Each flake a note, so pure and bright,
A crystalline dance in the serene night.
With every breath, the stillness sings,
Of ancient tales and winter's wings.

Time stands still in this embrace,
As magic paints the silent space.
The whispers glide on chilly air,
Inviting us to dream, to dare.

In every frozen shard we find,
The beauty woven, intertwined.
In enchanted stillness, joy ignites,
A symphony of snowy nights.

As dawn approaches, soft and sweet,
The harmonies of ice retreat.
Yet in our hearts, they will remain,
A melody of love's refrain.

Grace in the Whispering Snow

As snowflakes fall with gentle grace,
They cloak the world in soft embrace.
Whispers rustle through the trees,
In winter's breath, we find our peace.

Each flake a story, fresh and new,
A tapestry of silver hues.
We wander through this silent land,
With every step, hand in hand.

In twilight's glow, the magic stirs,
As nature's beauty softly blurs.
With every breath, we feel the chill,
Yet in our hearts, a warm thrill.

Amidst the snow, we laugh and play,
In muted colors, bright as day.
The world transforms, a lovely sight,
In winter's dance of purest white.

With every whisper, love will flow,
In graceful arcs of whispering snow.
Together, we will leave a mark,
A journey shared beneath the dark.

Eclipsed by a Blanket of White

The world draped softly in a veil,
Each branch adorned, a winter trail.
Silence wrapped the hills so tight,
Beneath the moon, all shimmers bright.

Footsteps muted, echoes faint,
Nature sighs, a silent paint.
The stars above seem to ignite,
In the hush of this tranquil night.

Frosted whispers dance with glee,
As snowflakes twirl wild and free.
A canvas pure, untouched and light,
Eclipsed by a blanket of white.

Shadows flicker in the glow,
Of distant lights, like dreams below.
In this charm, all worries fight,
To vanish deep from human sight.

A fleeting peace ensues the chills,
As warmth ignites in winter's drills.
With every breath, I feel so right,
Eclipsed by a blanket of white.

Whispers of the Frosty Air

Bright stars twinkling in the night,
Soft winds carry thoughts in flight.
Whispers weave through branches bare,
Tales of winter, light as air.

The breath of frost paints the trees,
Gentle murmurs ride the breeze.
Echoes of laughter, muffled cheer,
In the stillness, all draw near.

Moonlight bathes the world in grace,
Reflecting soft on every face.
In this hour, hearts are laid bare,
Embracing whispers of the frosty air.

Footsteps crunch on layers deep,
Awakening the dreams we keep.
Every flake a gem so rare,
In the beauty of the frosty air.

Time stands still, as if to pause,
In nature's grasp, there's no need for cause.
Wrapped in warmth, without a care,
We listen close to whispers rare.

Soft Luminescence Illuminating the Cold

A silver glow upon the land,
Soft luminescence, gentle hand.
Shadows dance with tender grace,
Enchanting all, this quiet space.

Twinkling lights from distant skies,
Glisten like dreams, a sweet surprise.
Each ray of hope, a story told,
Illuminating the cold.

Frosty breaths hang in the air,
Painting wonders for us to share.
In the stillness, night unfolds,
Magic beams and secrets hold.

Beneath the canopy of dark,
Every twinkle leaves its mark.
A soothing touch from stars so bold,
Soft luminescence, warming the cold.

As morning breaks, the dreams will fade,
Yet beauty lingers, softly laid.
Within our hearts, stories of old,
Live on in light, and in the cold.

Cocooned in Snowscape Serenity

Nestled within a snowy guise,
The world sleeps under starry skies.
Cocooned in warmth, so snug and tight,
Embraced by winter's quiet light.

Flakes fall gently, soft like sin,
Creating magic, peace within.
Each flurry swirls, a silent plea,
For moments held in harmony.

Branches heavy with the white,
A tapestry of pure delight.
Clouds drift lazily, dreams set free,
In this cocooned fragility.

Echoes whisper through the trees,
Carried by the crisp, cool breeze.
Comfort found in nature's spree,
Cocooned in snowscape serenity.

As twilight fades, and peace descends,
A sense of calm that never ends.
In winter's heart, we yearn to be,
Forever wrapped in harmony.

A Chill in the Starry Veil

Beneath the night's embrace, so cold,
Stars whisper secrets, dreams unfold.
In silver shadows, silence breathes,
The world lies still, and time deceives.

Frosty winds weave a quiet tune,
Under the watchful, glowing moon.
Each twinkle sparkles, softly bright,
Guiding wanderers through the night.

The air, a shiver, crisp and clear,
Echoes of laughter, drawing near.
In the distance, owls softly hoot,
Nature's rhythm, an ancient flute.

Wrapped in wonder, hearts ignite,
In the chill, warmth feels so right.
Stars align in a celestial dance,
Inviting lovers, lost in chance.

As dawn approaches, shadows flee,
In the light, a memory.
Yet still, beneath that starry dome,
The chill remains, a whispered home.

The Magic of Midnight's Caress

In midnight's arms, the world transforms,
Softly, the magic of silence warms.
A gentle breeze stirs the slumbering trees,
Whispering secrets in hushed degrees.

Moonlight drapes over the sleeping land,
Casting soft glow like a lover's hand.
Each shadow dances, embracing the night,
Painting the world in a silvery light.

Dreams take flight on this mystic breeze,
Carrying wishes across the seas.
With every heartbeat, the heavens sigh,
Under the spell of the midnight sky.

Stars twinkle bright in their velvet bed,
Guiding lost souls to where dreams are fed.
In this stillness, hearts find their place,
Enchanted forever by midnight's grace.

As dawn creeps in, the magic fades,
Yet in our hearts, the memory stayed.
For in each twilight, we'll seek to find,
The magic of midnight, forever entwined.

Dreaming Beneath a Winter's Cloak

Under a quilt of snow so white,
Stars twinkle softly, gleaming bright.
In the stillness, whispers roam,
Dreams gather close, a cozy home.

Trees stand tall, adorned in frost,
A peaceful beauty, never lost.
Snowflakes dance like soft ballet,
Drifting gently, drifting away.

Fires crackle in the hearth's warm glow,
Stories shared, as the cold winds blow.
Wrapped in blankets, hearts entwine,
In winter's charm, everything aligns.

Night blankets the world in tranquil grace,
Grateful smiles on each watching face.
In this season, time slows down,
In every flake, a magic crown.

Beneath the stars, we find our peace,
In winter's arms, all troubles cease.
Together we dream, as the night unfolds,
A winter's tale, forever retold.

Velvet Hush of the Falling Flakes

In the hush of night, snowflakes fall,
A velvet blanket covers all.
Softly they dance, a delicate flight,
Whispers of winter, pure and bright.

Gentle and quiet, they kiss the ground,
In their embrace, a muffled sound.
Echoes of laughter float on the breeze,
In winter's hold, hearts find their ease.

Each flake a story, unique, divine,
Falling like dreams in a perfect line.
Under the moon's watchful gaze,
The world transforms in a shimmering haze.

Children's laughter fills the air,
As snowmen rise with frosty care.
Layers of wonder cloak the day,
In flurries of joy, they dance and play.

As night unfolds, the stars appear,
In this tranquil beauty, we hold dear.
With every flake, a promise glows,
In winter's hush, love freely flows.

Glistening Silence Under Starlit Skies

In the stillness of the night,
Stars twinkle like secrets bright.
Whispers carried on the breeze,
Nature's calm, a soothing tease.

Crickets sing their lullabies,
Echoes under velvet skies.
Moonbeams dance on tranquil streams,
Filling hearts with hopeful dreams.

Shadows stretch in silver light,
Tales unfold in soft twilight.
Night embraces, pure and clear,
In this moment, all is dear.

Thoughts drift like the clouds above,
Wrapped in peace, surrounded by love.
Each heartbeat slows, each breath a sigh,
Underneath the endless sky.

Glistening silence softly glows,
As the world in slumber grows.
In this haven, time stands still,
A quiet world, a heart to fill.

Quietude of the Frosted Night

Frosted branches shimmer bright,
Blankets soft in shades of white.
Silent whispers fill the air,
Winter's breath is everywhere.

Stars like diamonds softly gleam,
In the hush, the night's a dream.
Every flake a story told,
In this world, both calm and cold.

Gentle winds begin to sigh,
As the moon floats in the sky.
Nature sleeps under the glow,
In a realm, calm and slow.

Footprints left on icy ground,
In this peace, the heart is found.
Quietude of night so deep,
In stillness, winter's secrets keep.

Wrapped in layers, warm and tight,
Feel the magic of the night.
In the frost, our spirits dance,
Embraced by winter's charming trance.

A Shroud of White Beneath the Moon

A shroud of white, the world sleeps tight,
Beneath the gaze of the full moon's light.
Snowflakes drift and softly fall,
Blanketing the earth, a wondrous thrall.

In the stillness, beauty reigns,
Touching hearts, softening pains.
Twinkling stars through branches peek,
In this night, the silence speaks.

Echoes of the past reside,
In the quiet, memories abide.
The moon whispers, secrets spun,
Guiding dreams till night is done.

Each breath of cold, a fleeting kiss,
Wrapped in winter's snowy bliss.
Night embraces in its bright hue,
A canvas painted fresh and new.

A shroud of white, a world reborn,
In the silence, hope is worn.
Underneath this silver spell,
In the still, our hearts can dwell.

Whispers of Winter's Gentle Touch

Whispers of winter, soft and near,
In the chill, the heart can hear.
Snowflakes dance on fragrant air,
Every sigh a gentle prayer.

Frosty breath against the pane,
Tales of joy, of loss, of gain.
In the hush, the world unwinds,
In this magic, peace we find.

Candles flicker, shadows play,
As twilight slowly drifts away.
Wrapped in warmth, the fires glow,
In this moment, love will grow.

Silhouettes of trees, so grand,
Against the white, they proudly stand.
Whispers linger on the breeze,
Carried softly through the trees.

Winter's touch, a tender grace,
In its arms, we find our place.
Amongst the snow, our spirits rise,
Awakened by the starlit skies.

Veils of Frost on Slumbering Streets

Veils of frost cling to the air,
Silent whispers, winter's care.
Trees stand tall, dressed in white,
Underneath the moon's soft light.

Footsteps muffled on the ground,
Where the heart of night is found.
Streetlamps glow like distant stars,
Guiding souls through gentle scars.

Each breath hangs in the chilly night,
A canvas of a world so bright.
Crystal branches bend and sway,
In the hush of winter's play.

Windows glow with warmth inside,
While the frost outside does bide.
Every home a glowing beacon,
In the calm, the heart's sweet beacon.

Nature sleeps beneath the chill,
All is quiet, all is still.
In the stillness, dreams take flight,
Veils of frost in soft moonlight.

Winter's Grace in the Stillness

In the stillness, time slows down,
Covered fields wear a crystal crown.
Silent echoes in the trees,
Drifting whispers in the breeze.

Snowflakes dance with gentle grace,
Filling all the empty space.
Softly landing, pure and white,
Turning dark to soft delight.

The world adorned in silver hues,
Nature's palette, peaceful views.
Footprints leave a fleeting mark,
In the glow of evening's spark.

Stars peek through the velvet sky,
Twinkling softly as they fly.
In this night of calm and cheer,
Winter's grace is ever near.

Whispers flow like silent streams,
Wrapped in winter's tender dreams.
In the stillness, hearts align,
Finding solace, yours and mine.

Sparkling Shadows of Nightfall

Shadows weave as daylight fades,
In the dusk, the magic glades.
Stars awaken, soft and bright,
Sparkling gently, pure delight.

Whispers haunt the silent air,
Filling spaces, everywhere.
Every corner holds a dream,
In the dusk's enchanting scheme.

Beneath the sky's deep, dreamy blue,
Twinkling lights in shadows grew.
Nightfall cradles the escaping sun,
A dance of worlds entwined as one.

Moonbeams play on surfaces bare,
Casting glimmers, cold yet fair.
The night unveils its soft embrace,
Woven threads of time and space.

In every heart, a secret grows,
Where the night's soft magic flows.
Sparkling shadows hold the key,
To the dreams that set us free.

The Embrace of Quiet Flurries

The world in white, so softly dressed,
Gentle flurries find their rest.
Caressing branches, the ground below,
In winter's arms, they gently flow.

Whispers of the snowflakes play,
Each one unique, a ballet.
Laughter dances upon the breeze,
Nature's gift, a moment's tease.

Quiet flurries fill the air,
Wrapping all in love and care.
A soft embrace, a tender touch,
In their presence, we feel so much.

Evening settles, all is bright,
Underneath the starlit night.
Snowflakes twirl in a soft waltz,
Nature's beauty, never false.

In every heart, a spark ignites,
As flurries dance in soft delights.
Embracing winter's gentle song,
In their arms, we all belong.

Dreams Weaved in Winter's Embrace

In the hush of falling snow,
Whispers dance on frozen air.
Each flake, a dream we let go,
Caught in winter's gentle stare.

Beneath the frost where shadows play,
Silence cradles hopes so dear.
Winter wraps the world in gray,
Yet, in stillness, dreams appear.

Luminous stars break the night,
Casting glimmers, soft and bright.
Embers warm our heart's delight,
In this season, pure and white.

We gather close, our stories shared,
Underneath the moon's soft glow.
In this moment, hearts are bared,
In winter's arms, love's warmth we know.

As dawn awakens, dreams take flight,
Painting skies with colors bold.
In the embrace of winter's night,
Hope and joy forever hold.

An Ode to the Night's White Canvas

The moon spills silver on the ground,
A canvas vast, a tranquil space.
In this quiet, magic's found,
As shadows dance with gentle grace.

Stars like diamonds pierce the dark,
Every twinkle tells a tale.
Whispers echo, leaving mark,
In this night where dreams prevail.

With each breath, the world stands still,
A symphony of peace unfolds.
In the silence, hearts can fill,
With secrets that the night beholds.

The chill embraces, crisp and clear,
Wrapping souls as soft as lace.
In the stillness, we draw near,
To the warmth of night's embrace.

On this canvas, pure and bright,
We find our hopes, our futures cast.
An ode to dreams that take flight,
On this canvas, shadows past.

Tales Rendered in the Winter's Glow

Fires flicker in the night,
Casting warmth on frosted glass.
Tales emerge in glowing light,
While winter's chill begins to pass.

Gathered round, we share our lore,
Each tale woven with care.
In the heart, we keep the score,
Of moments we hold rare.

Blankets wrapped and laughter flows,
Echoes ring of past delight.
As the chill outside bestows,
A world dressed in shimmering white.

With each story, hearts ignite,
Bringing joy to coldest days.
In winter's glow, we unite,
Finding warmth in woven ways.

As ember's spark fades into dawn,
The tales linger in the air.
In winter's glow, we are reborn,
Heartfelt memories we all share.

Sculpted Silence Beneath the Stars

In the stillness of the night,
Underneath a quilt of skies,
Silence breathes with pure delight,
As we gaze where starlight lies.

Each twinkle, a whispered dream,
Carved in darkness, vivid, bright.
In this vast and tranquil scheme,
All our worries take to flight.

The world below sleeps tight and sound,
While the cosmos plays its part.
In the depth, our hopes are found,
Sculpted whispers touch the heart.

Through the night, we connect deep,
In this peaceful, starry trance.
Keeping dreams that we shall keep,
In the night's enchanting dance.

As dawn approaches with its glow,
The stars fade to a gentle morn.
Yet the silence we bestow,
Lives within us, softly worn.

The Dance of Snowflakes Under Starlight

Gentle flakes fall from the sky,
Whirling softly, floating by.
Underneath the glowing light,
They twirl and spin, a pure delight.

Each one unique, a fragile grace,
Touching softly every place.
A silent waltz, the world awakes,
In this dance that winter makes.

Beneath the stars, they forge a path,
Creating beauty in their bath.
Nature's art in winter's chill,
A moment captured, time stands still.

Listen closely, hear them sing,
In the stillness, joy they bring.
Softly whispering dreams untold,
As night unfolds, the magic holds.

The dance of snowflakes, ethereal flight,
Painting the world in shades of white.
A fleeting glimpse of winter's heart,
In the starlight, they play their part.

Echoes of Chill Beneath the Night Sky

In the stillness, cold winds sigh,
Whispers carried, passing by.
Legacy of winter's breath,
Echoes linger, tales of death.

Stars alight in velvet sea,
Each a watcher, wild and free.
Beneath the sky so vast and deep,
Silence cradles dreams in sleep.

Frosty fingers touch the ground,
In their grasp, no warmth is found.
A shiver runs through hoary trees,
The night hums soft with winter's freeze.

Footsteps crunch on snowbitten ways,
While shadows dance in moonlit plays.
Echoes of chill whisper low,
Carrying stories of frost and snow.

Blankets of white, the earth's embrace,
Time moves slow in this frozen space.
Under the watchful, starry eye,
Winter's breath, a lullaby.

Lullabies of the Frozen Air

Softly sings the winter breeze,
Lullabies through barren trees.
Wrapped in slumber, earth complies,
Underneath the starlit skies.

Frozen whispers, tales of old,
Stories shared, like dreams retold.
Each breath dances in the cold,
A magic woven, pure and bold.

Gentle hush enfolds the night,
Moonbeams drape in silver light.
Wrapped in warmth from nature's hand,
Lullabies across the land.

Snowflakes drift on unseen wings,
Nature's choir in quiet sings.
Echoing in the frosty air,
Every note, a soft, sweet prayer.

Rest now, world, in silent peace,
Let the lullabies never cease.
In the stillness, find your dream,
Winter's essence, pure as cream.

Celestial Frost on Darkened Streets

Moonlight dances on the ground,
Crowned in frost, the world is found.
Stars and shadows come to play,
On darkened streets, they softly sway.

Glistening crystals light the night,
Painting pathways, pure and bright.
Each step taken is a song,
In this place where dreams belong.

Whispers echo through the trees,
Carried along by winter's breeze.
Celestial frost paints the town,
In this darkness, wear your crown.

Silence wraps the world in grace,
Every heart finds its own space.
Underneath the watchful stars,
Journey forth, erase the scars.

Through the frost, the night unveils,
Magic hidden in the trails.
Celestial wonders, bittersweet,
The beauty lies beneath our feet.

Serenity Cloaked in Frosty Beauty

In the hush of dawn's first light,
Whispers dance on icy air,
Trees wear coats of frosty white,
Nature's beauty, calm and rare.

Crystal blooms on every leaf,
Silent magic, pure and bright,
Moments ponder, deep belief,
In the stillness, hearts take flight.

Rivers wrapped in silver lace,
Flowing softly, sweet and slow,
Gentle echoes, winter's grace,
In this realm, all worries go.

Footsteps leave a fleeting trace,
Shadows dance with fleeting light,
In this sacred, tranquil place,
Serenity, pure and white.

As the world takes a deep breath,
Nature sleeps beneath the sky,
In this moment, life meets death,
Frosty beauty, soft goodbye.

Silent Streets Dressed in Pearl

Moonlit paths so quiet lie,
Wrapped in veils of shimmering glow,
Every echo whispers, sigh,
Magic flows through depths below.

Footsteps muffled by the night,
Secret tales the shadows weave,
Pearl-like droplets catch the light,
In their shimmer, hearts believe.

Windows gleam like distant stars,
Guarding dreams that softly sleep,
A world held in midnight's bars,
Silent streets where secrets keep.

Gentle whispers from the sky,
As the frost begins to weave,
In these moments, soft and shy,
Winter's breath begins to cleave.

Each corner holds a quiet truth,
Stories linger in the air,
Jewel-like glimmers, ghosts of youth,
Silent streets, a tranquil prayer.

The Gentle Touch of Winter's Breath

Winter's breath, a soft caress,
Whispers waltzing through the trees,
Blankets draped in soft finesse,
Wrapping earth in gentle freeze.

Snowflakes twirl like whispered dreams,
Each one unique, a fleeting song,
Nature's quilt, a pure-sewn seam,
In this stillness, we belong.

Frozen streams in quiet pools,
Mirroring the starlit skies,
In their depths, eternal schools,
Where the heart of winter lies.

The world slowed down, a tender sigh,
Breath of winter, slow and sweet,
In each [howling](https://en.wiktionary.org/wiki/howling)
wind that passes by,
Nature's lullaby, complete.

As the sun begins to rise,
Painting gold on frosty white,
Winter's touch, a pure disguise,
Turns to warmth, from cold of night.

Glittering Pillows Beneath the Starry Dome

Underneath the velvet sky,
Pillows made of glistening light,
Each star a whisper floating by,
Wrapped in dreams of endless night.

Fingers trace the cosmic glow,
Sparkling jewels, nature's art,
In this garden, soft and slow,
Every twinkle heals the heart.

Moonbeams dance on sleepy hills,
Casting shadows, soft and long,
In the stillness, magic fills,
Every creature hums a song.

Breathing in this cool night air,
Feeling peace in every breath,
Softly woven, sweet despair,
In these moments, love finds depth.

As the night unveils its charms,
Wrapped in peace, we drift away,
Under blankets, safe and warm,
In the night's embrace, we stay.

The Nocturnal Embrace of Winter

The moon hangs low and bright,
Casting shadows in the night.
Whispers of the icy breeze,
Dancing through the barren trees.

Snowflakes fall like gentle sighs,
Blanketing the world, it lies.
Stars twinkle with a silver grace,
In winter's cold and quiet space.

A hushed stillness fills the air,
Nature wrapped in frosty care.
Nighttime's beauty, stark yet true,
In the embrace of winter's hue.

Footprints trace a path divine,
In the white where shadows dine.
Every step a soft refrain,
Echoes of a tranquil plain.

The world is hushed, a gentle balm,
A scene that captures hearts, so calm.
In winter's arms, we find retreat,
A solace wrapped in chilly sheet.

Shimmering Veil of Crystal Dreams

In the quiet of the night,
Stars weave dreams with soft light.
Crystals spark in moonlight's glow,
As if time itself moves slow.

A tapestry of silken white,
Whispers of the fleeting night.
Each flake a wish, a story spun,
In the gleaming dance of fun.

Glistening paths beneath our feet,
Magic lingers, bittersweet.
In this realm of frozen sighs,
Hope and wonder softly rise.

The veil of dreams, a gentle lace,
Cocooning all in warm embrace.
With every step, a promise made,
In winter's spell, we shall not fade.

Underneath the starlit dome,
Crystal dreams, our hearts, they comb.
In this shimmering, wondrous stream,
Life unfolds in whispered dream.

Soft Footfalls in the Whispering Snow

Footfalls echo through the night,
Snowflakes swirl, a pure delight.
Each step taken, soft and kind,
In the silence, peace we find.

Winter's breath caresses slow,
Gentle whispers, quiet flow.
Nature's chorus, sweet and low,
Guides us through the silent glow.

Hushed serene, the world stands still,
In the night, we feel the thrill.
With every breath, a moment's grace,
Soft reminders of this place.

Branches bow beneath the weight,
Of sparkling dreams that softly grate.
In this wonder, hearts unite,
With each footfall, purest light.

A snow-clad world, so fresh and new,
Invites us forth with skies so blue.
In whispered tones, we're drawn to play,
In winter's arms, we drift away.

Twilight's Silver Canvas

As daylight fades, the colors blend,
Twilight whispers, day will end.
Shadows stretch and softly sigh,
Embracing dusk as night draws nigh.

The sky adorned in purple hue,
A masterpiece that feels so true.
Stars appear, like gems on high,
Against the canvas of the sky.

In the stillness, dreams take flight,
A lullaby in fading light.
Nature holds her breath in awe,
At twilight's charm, we can't ignore.

The silver glow, a soothing balm,
Wrapping the world in tender calm.
In shades of blue and softest gray,
We greet the night, we find our way.

With every heartbeat, shadows weave,
In twilight's grace, we learn to believe.
A world transformed, serene, and bright,
In the painting of the night.

Frosted Trees in Whispered Light

Beneath the boughs, the silence weaves,
A tapestry of dreams and leaves.
The frost hangs low, a shivering breath,
In twilight's glow, we dance with death.

Each branch adorned, a glistening crown,
In winter's grace, the world slows down.
Whispers linger, soft and serene,
As shadows play in silver sheen.

Footprints trace through frozen dew,
A symphony, old but ever new.
In frosted realms, we wander free,
Lost in a spell, just you and me.

The hush enfolds the night in peace,
As time and tide find sweet release.
Together here, where soft winds sigh,
Beneath the kiss of a starlit sky.

Awake, the dreams of winter's hold,
As stories in the frost unfold.
In whispered light, our spirits gleam,
Among the trees, we chase the dream.

Twilight's Cascade of Frost

As twilight drapes in hues so deep,
The world around seems fast asleep.
A cascade falls, the icy lace,
Embracing night with sweet embrace.

Moonlight dances on frozen streams,
Where shadows weave our secret dreams.
Each breath a plume in frosty air,
We twirl like dancers unaware.

The stars are born, a twinkling song,
In this enchanted place, we belong.
With every flake that gently falls,
A hush descends, and magic calls.

The horizon glows, a line of fire,
While whispers pulse with soft desire.
In winter's grip, our hearts ignite,
With warmth that beats against the night.

Through canopies of sparkling white,
We wander on 'neath the moon's soft light.
In twilight's arms, we ever trust,
With nature's frost, our dreams adjust.

Stars Cradled in a White Lullaby

In blankets white, the world is hushed,
A lullaby where stillness brushed.
Stars twinkle down from heights above,
Cradled gently, wrapped in love.

Each crystal flake a tender sigh,
That tells the tales of winter's eye.
The night unfolds its velvet hue,
As dreams awaken, fresh and new.

Time suspends in frosted glow,
Where whispered secrets drift and flow.
With every breath, the echoes blend,
In winter's arms, our hearts will mend.

The shimmer sings a soothing tune,
Guided softly by the moon.
In gentle hands, we find repose,
As night wraps round and silence grows.

Awake in wonder, lost in light,
With stars alive in velvet night.
Together here, our spirits share,
A peaceful bond, a loving pair.

Hushed Echoes of Winter's Song

In twilight's breath, the echoes flow,
An ancient song, both soft and slow.
With every note, the chill ignites,
While winter wraps the world in white.

A melody of frost and peace,
Where beauty dwells and sorrows cease.
Through branches bare, the whispers call,
In nature's arms, we cherish all.

Each flake that falls, a gentle grace,
A fleeting glimpse of time and space.
From dusk to dawn, our spirits rise,
In harmony with starlit skies.

The echoes weave through silent trees,
With every pause, the heart believes.
Amid the cold, we find the light,
As winter's breath wraps us in night.

Together here, where silence sings,
We dance with joy in frosty rings.
With hushed echoes, the night belongs,
To us, enchanted by winter's song.

Eclipsed by the Season's Breath

The trees stand tall and bare,
A whisper in the chilling air.
Leaves have danced, now they rest,
Nature's pause, it feels like a test.

Clouds blanket the sun's warm embrace,
Winter's breath upon my face.
Silent echoes shape the land,
A tranquil touch, a gentle hand.

Footprints mark a snowy trail,
Guiding dreams where shadows pale.
Footsteps soft, a muted sound,
In this hush, peace is found.

Time meanders, slow and kind,
Within this quiet, solace bind.
Eclipsed in frost, I close my eyes,
Let winter's lullaby arise.

In the stillness, hope does dwell,
Through whispered winds, a tale to tell.
Seasons shift, yet still we stand,
Eclipsed by beauty, hand in hand.

Night's Paintbrush on a Frozen Palette

The moon dips low, a silver hue,
Brushes strokes of night anew.
Stars twinkle bright, a dazzling sight,
Each one a tale, a spark of light.

Canvas vast, the sky unfolds,
Whispers of secrets the darkness holds.
A dance of shadows, soft and bold,
In the chill, stories whispered and told.

Frozen lakes mirror the sky,
Where dreams and reality softly lie.
Each star a wish that travels far,
Guided by the night's own star.

The air is crisp, alive with peace,
In these moments, worries cease.
Nature's art, a quiet grace,
In the dark, a warm embrace.

Through night's brush, imagination flows,
A realm where endless wonder grows.
In stillness, we find our way,
Night's masterpiece holds sway.

Echoes of Serenity in Twinkling White

Snowflakes fall, a gentle dance,
In their presence, there's a trance.
Each flake shines like a star's glow,
Whispering secrets, soft and slow.

The world transforms, a canvas bright,
Cradled in winter's silken light.
A hush envelops, calm and clear,
Echoes of peace draw us near.

Children laugh, their joy takes flight,
Adventures born in pure delight.
Snowmen rise with carrot nose,
In this land where wonder flows.

Footsteps crunch on a frosty path,
Nature's charm leads us to laugh.
In this realm, both vast and small,
We find our hearts entwined with all.

A moment held, time stands still,
In the white, we chase the thrill.
Echoes linger, sweet and bright,
In serenity's embrace tonight.

Beneath the Silver Stars We Wander

The night unfolds a vast embrace,
Beneath the stars, we find our place.
Whispers of wind guide our feet,
In starlit paths, our hearts will meet.

Constellations spark the darkened sky,
Telling tales of worlds gone by.
Each twinkle a dream, a wish bestowed,
In cosmic dance, our spirits flowed.

Moonlit glow on the tranquil lake,
Reflections shimmer, softly wake.
With every breath, we feel the space,
In the still, we find our grace.

Time meanders in this light,
Every heartbeat feels so right.
Beneath the silver, hand in hand,
We chart our dreams upon this land.

Moments linger, etched in night,
In the shadows, hearts take flight.
Beneath the stars, we wander free,
In this vastness, just you and me.

Crystal-Studded Dreams Beneath the Night

In the silence of night, they gleam,
Jewels scattered like whispers, a dream.
Moonlight dances on silver leaves,
Painting shadows where the heart believes.

Stars twinkle like secrets, profound,
Each one holds a wish tightly bound.
The world slumbers in a soft embrace,
Lost in the depths of time and space.

Whispers of hope in the cool night air,
Tales of old linger everywhere.
With hearts wide open, we softly tread,
In this realm where dreams are bred.

Every sparkle a story, untold yet clear,
Inviting the souls who wander near.
We close our eyes, let our spirits soar,
In this place, we forever explore.

Beneath a canopy of dreams we align,
Crystal-studded visions intertwine.
A sacred moment, both tender and bright,
In the stillness, we bathe in the night.

An Evening Cloaked in Snowy Mirth

The world dons a blanket, soft and white,
Whispers of winter dance in the light.
Laughter echoes down frosty lanes,
As joy is woven in snowy chains.

Children twirl 'neath the lazy flakes,
Building dreams as the world awakes.
Snowmen rise with their carrot noses,
Gentle joys that the cold exposes.

Twinkling lights adorn the trees,
While the air carries sweet melodies.
With every breath, a cloud of steam,
As warmth and laughter stitch the seam.

The evening wraps us in its embrace,
Soft snowflakes dancing, a gentle grace.
Footprints marking the joy we sow,
Creating memories in the glow.

Let this moment linger, sweet and bright,
In the magic of a snowy night.
Together we share in winter's cheer,
As the world sparkles, our hearts sincere.

A Chilling Waltz Under Starry Skies

Beneath the stars, we glide and sway,
The chill wraps tight, but we feel okay.
In the quiet night, our spirits sing,
As winter whispers the joy it brings.

Each flake that falls is a song anew,
In a bittersweet dance, just me and you.
The sky gleams bright with a celestial spark,
Guiding us through shadows, leaving a mark.

Hands entwined, we twirl in the cold,
Stories of love in the moonlight told.
Breath like steam, we exhale a dream,
In this winter waltz, we're more than a team.

The night unfolds with each graceful turn,
In the icy air, our hearts brightly burn.
Together we spin, under cosmic delight,
A chilling waltz that feels so right.

With every dance step, we chase away fear,
In the quietude, all that's dear.
Stars are our partners, the moon our guide,
In this beautiful waltz, we forever abide.

The Allure of Winter's Embrace

A world transformed, cloaked in white,
Winter whispers in the light.
Branches bend with a frosty touch,
Nature's canvas, we admire so much.

With every breath, serenity found,
Quiet moments in peace abound.
Snowflakes twirl like ballerinas bold,
In their elegance, stories unfold.

The crackling fire, warmth inside,
Where memories linger, and hearts abide.
Hot cocoa swirls with marshmallow skies,
In these treasured moments, our spirit flies.

Outside, the chill invites us to play,
As laughter dances in the light of day.
Snowball fights and sleds racing down,
In the joy of winter, we wear a crown.

Embraced by the season, we find our place,
In the beauty of winter's gentle grace.
With hearts all aglow, we savor the tease,
Of winter's allure, a constant breeze.

Gliding Through the Frosted Air

Beneath a sky, so pale and bright,
The air is crisp, a pure delight.
With every breath, the frost does sing,
A chilly thrill, a gentle wing.

Trees adorned in icy lace,
Nature's art, a tranquil space.
Footprints crunch on a winter's ground,
As whispers of the snow abound.

The world wrapped in a silvery glow,
Soft flurries dance, a quiet show.
In this moment, time does pause,
Held in winter's tender cause.

The breath of night, so fresh and clear,
Echoes softly, drawing near.
Stars twinkle like distant flames,
Guiding hearts with no demands.

So gliding through this frosted air,
Life's magic breathes without a care.
With each soft step, we find our way,
In winter's charm that holds us sway.

Invisible Symphony of Snowflakes

In twilight's hush, the snowflakes fall,
An unseen tune, a silent call.
Whispers weave through the frozen night,
A melody wrapped in purest white.

Each flake unique, a fleeting grace,
Dances softly in time and space.
They twirl and spin, so light, so free,
A symphony played for you and me.

The ground awaits, a quilt unwound,
As secrets of the sky are crowned.
A wonder stirs, the world aglow,
In this magic, life starts to flow.

Cold breaths mingle with starry dreams,
The night is full of gentle themes.
Beneath this veil, we search and seek,
For warmth that lies in hearts so meek.

The music swells, then fades away,
As dawn's first light claims the day.
But in our souls, the echoes stay,
An invisible symphony at play.

Crystalline Dreams in the Sudden Chill

The frost arrives, a sudden chill,
Painting landscapes with a thrill.
Crystalline dreams in the frosty air,
Whispers of winter's quiet care.

Each branch adorned with diamonds bright,
Shimmers softly in morning light.
A world transformed, so calm, so still,
Held in the magic of winter's will.

Footsteps crunch on a path untold,
As stories of the season unfold.
In every breath a spark ignites,
Moments cherished on breezy nights.

Through the woods where shadows play,
Winter's breath leads the way.
With hearts aglow, we wander near,
In crystalline dreams, we hold dear.

As twilight falls, the world breathes slow,
Wrapped in peace, a gentle flow.
In winter's grasp, we find release,
Crystalline dreams bring sweet, sweet peace.

The Night's Cloak of Pearly Whispers

A cloak of night, so dark and deep,
Holds secrets that the stars shall keep.
Pearly whispers kiss the ground,
In the silence, magic's found.

The moonlight spills, a silken thread,
Across the world where shadows tread.
Each glimmer soft, a tale to tell,
In the quiet, all is well.

Snowflakes fall like whispers sweet,
Softly blanketing our feet.
In this hush, the heart can soar,
Finding peace forevermore.

The chilly breeze brings dreams alive,
In winter's arms, we thrive and strive.
Underneath the night's gentle sweep,
We find our courage, we take a leap.

The world transformed, a canvas bright,
Shadows blend, and hearts take flight.
Within the night, we deeply sigh,
A cloak of whispers, we drift by.

The Canvas of Night Laces with Frost

Stars twinkle like jewels bright,
On a canvas draped in night.
Whispers of the chilling breeze,
Dance through branches of the trees.

Moonlight spills in silver streams,
Igniting all the waking dreams.
Each flake falls with softest grace,
Bathe the world in icy lace.

The night wears a cloak of blue,
With crystalline wonders anew.
In the stillness, magic weaves,
Stories that the heart believes.

A tranquil hush envelops all,
As the frosty night does call.
Silhouettes in shadowed flight,
Embrace the beauty of the night.

A Serene Dreamscape in White

Blanket of snow on the ground,
In this silence, calm is found.
Softly twirls the drifting flakes,
Creating dreams that winter makes.

Whispers echo through the trees,
Carried gently by the breeze.
Footprints marked in purest white,
Lead us deeper into night.

Moonbeams dance on powdered hills,
Each caress, a soft thrill.
A world transformed, a treasure,
The serene heart finds its measure.

Frozen breath in crisp, cool air,
Nature's beauty everywhere.
In this dreamscape, time stands still,
A serene charm, a gentle thrill.

Reflections of Beauty in Frosted Glows

Underneath the glowing skies,
Frosted light, a sweet surprise.
Crystal trees in quiet peace,
In their beauty, all fears cease.

Morning dew on petals bright,
Sparkles in the pale daylight.
Nature's art, a wondrous show,
In reflections, love will grow.

Glistening fields invite the heart,
Every glance, a work of art.
In this moment, time flows slow,
Captured in the frosted glow.

With each breath, we find our place,
Embraced in winter's soft embrace.
Reflections of a truth so clear,
Beauty breathed into our sphere.

A Silent Reverie Wrapped in White

A soft blanket cloaks the land,
Whispers held in gentle hand.
Snowflakes fall like silent sighs,
Kissing earth as stillness lies.

In the hush, dreams intertwine,
Wrapped in warmth, your heart is mine.
The world in white, a story told,
In every flake, a truth unfolds.

Gentle murmurs, soft and light,
Guide us through the chilly night.
With each step, a path we trace,
In this reverie, warm embrace.

Frozen moments, sweet and pure,
In this peace, we find our cure.
A silent ode to love's delight,
Wrapped together, hearts ignited.

Slumbering Earth in Soft Embrace

Beneath the stars, the earth does sigh,
Wrapped in blankets, low and nigh.
The whispers of the wind do play,
As night slips softly into gray.

The trees stand tall, their branches bare,
Guarding secrets in the air.
The moonlight dances on the ground,
In this hushed night, peace is found.

Creatures stir in quiet bliss,
In shadows deep, they find their kiss.
Awake, asleep, all in one,
Under the gaze of the wandering sun.

Dreams entangle in gentle threads,
While the world rests its weary heads.
The heartbeat of the earth so slow,
In silent nights, life starts to flow.

In soft embrace, the night unfolds,
With stories waiting to be told.
The slumbering earth in twilight's glow,
Holds secrets deep, forever low.

Veil of Dreams in the Cool Air

In twilight's shade, the dreams descend,
In cool air, their whispers blend.
Stars weave tales of love and fate,
As night surrounds, they gently wait.

A breeze carries the scent of hope,
Where shadows play and spirits cope.
The veil of dreams, a silken thread,
Weaves through the thoughts that dance in threads.

Moonlight bathes the world in peace,
With every sigh, the worries cease.
In quiet moments, hearts align,
Beneath the sky, so vast, divine.

Caught in reveries, sweet and light,
We drift on waves of dreamy flight.
In soft embraces, we suspend,
Our fears gone wild, our hearts unbend.

The cool air cradles, holds us tight,
As dreams take wing in the velvet night.
With every breath, we find our way,
In this enchanted, starry play.

Celestial Snowflakes Falling Softly

In winter's hush, the snowflakes fall,
Each a whisper, a gentle call.
They dance like feathers from the sky,
In a graceful waltz, they drift and fly.

Blanketing earth in a quilt of white,
Transforming the world, a wondrous sight.
They catch the light with a spark divine,
Each flake unique, a fleeting sign.

The silence deepens, a dreamlike hue,
As nature pauses, bathed anew.
The cold air sparkles with whispered tales,
In a world where wonder never fails.

In quiet moments, time does slow,
As celestial flakes begin to glow.
They linger softly on every bough,
A fleeting magic in each quiet vow.

With every flake, a story told,
Of winter's charm, both brave and bold.
In the stillness, hearts embrace,
As celestial snowflakes find their place.

The Stillness of a Chilling Hour

Amidst the chill, the world holds still,
Each breath a cloud, thick and shrill.
The hour dips in shadows long,
In silence deep, we find our song.

Frosted whispers grace the air,
In the stillness, we find a prayer.
The moon, a sentinel so bright,
Watches over the canvas of night.

Life pauses in this sacred space,
Time unfolds with gentle grace.
Each heartbeat echoes in the dark,
Creating warmth, a tender spark.

In the chilling hour, dreams arise,
Painting visions where hope lies.
With every shiver, a tale begins,
In the stillness, the heart always wins.

As stars twinkle in an inky sea,
We find our peace, so wild and free.
In the embrace of this cooling hour,
Love blooms forth, a radiant flower.

The Still Dreaming in the Hour of Ice

The night breathes soft with icy hush,
As dreams take flight on a silver rush.
Beneath the stars in a glistening trance,
Whispers of winter weave their dance.

In stillness draped, the world feels bright,
Snowflakes fall like whispers of light.
Each shimmering flake tells a tale,
Of quiet moments that gently unveil.

Frozen branches bow in grace,
Caught in a dream, this tranquil space.
Time lingers long, as shadows play,
In the still dreaming of night's soft sway.

Echoes of silence paint the air,
With gentle breaths, we softly share.
In the hour where dreams intertwine,
We find our peace, where stars align.

As dawn peeks in on fragile light,
The hour of ice bids us goodnight.
But still, we hold the dreams so dear,
In the still dreaming of winter near.

Silent Whispers of Winter Night

Beneath the veil of the deep night sky,
Silent whispers of winter sigh.
Snowflakes dance like secrets untold,
In the hush of darkness, soft and bold.

Moonlight bathes the world in white,
Guiding dreams through the starry night.
Each breath of cold, a tender sigh,
In the stillness, our hopes fly high.

Footsteps muffled on the snowy ground,
Echoes of peace are all around.
With every heartbeat, the world slows down,
In silent whispers, we quietly drown.

Frosted windows with tales to share,
Of quiet moments and soothing care.
Under the stars, we find our way,
In the stillness of night's gentle sway.

As dawn approaches with waves of gold,
The silent whispers begin to unfold.
Yet in our hearts, they hold the light,
Of winter's beauty in the depth of night.

Frost-kissed Dreams in the Moonlight

Under the glow of the silver moon,
Frost-kissed dreams begin to bloom.
Each crystal glimmers, a wish in the dark,
Painting the night with a magical spark.

The world turns quiet, bathed in white,
Where shadows dance in dreamy light.
In the silent chill, we find our song,
In frost-kissed dreams, we all belong.

Branches wear coats of shimmering ice,
As stars above twinkle like paradise.
In hushed corners, our hopes ignite,
With frosty breath, we chase the night.

Every gust carries whispers of cheer,
Embraced by winter's arms, sincere.
In moonlit realms, our spirits soar,
Frost-kissed dreams forevermore.

And as the night gives way to dawn,
Our dreams stay nestled, though we yawn.
In this embrace of the cold and bright,
Frost-kissed dreams guide our flight.

A Blanket of White Silence

A blanket of white settles low,
Softly covering the world below.
Each flake whispers a gentle tale,
Of winter's heart in a frosty veil.

Underneath the still starry dome,
The silence whispers us softly home.
Where shadows linger in soft embrace,
A blanket of white, a tranquil space.

Footsteps print on the world's white score,
Each step a promise, a wish to explore.
In the hush, we find our way,
Beneath the stars, where dreams play.

The air is crisp, each breath draws near,
Wrapped in the magic of winter's sphere.
With every sound, the stillness sings,
A blanket of silence, the peace it brings.

As daylight breaks, the world ignites,
But in our hearts, the quiet delights.
For even in noise, we can feel,
The blanket of white, grounding and real.

Serenade of Flakes in the Dark

Whispers of snow drift softly down,
Kissing the earth with a frosty crown.
Moonlight dances on the frozen ground,
In this stillness, magic is found.

Stars peek through the velvet night,
Guiding the flakes with gentle light.
Each flake unique, a tale untold,
In chilly air, their beauty unfolds.

The night breathes calm, so rich and deep,
While all around, the world is asleep.
Echoes of laughter, faint and bright,
Carried on winds of winter's flight.

Underneath trees with branches bare,
Silence weaves through the crisp, cool air.
A serenade of flakes in the dark,
An enchanting whisper, a silvery spark.

As dawn breaks softly, shadows will fade,
Leaving behind this serene cascade.
Yet in our hearts, it forever remains,
The serenade sung by frost-laden chains.

Waltz of Ice Beneath a Glistening Sky

Beneath the sky, a canvas so bright,
Ice crystals waltz in the morning light.
They spin and twirl, a delicate dance,
In this frosty realm, a perfect romance.

The air is crisp, each breath a cloud,
Nature's beauty, both humble and proud.
Sunbeams glisten on each icy wing,
A winter's lullaby, joy to bring.

Through the branches, shadows play,
Harmonious whispers of the day.
Each flake that falls, a graceful tease,
In this waltz of ice, the heart finds ease.

Glistening landscapes stretch far and wide,
In every corner, the magic does hide.
Nature's palette, serene and grand,
Here in the wonder, we take our stand.

When twilight falls and the stars awaken,
The dance continues, never forsaken.
Waltz of ice beneath a glistening sky,
In the silence, our spirits fly.

Frozen Echoes in a Silent World

In a world draped in white and still,
Echoes of winter touch the hill.
Footprints mark a journey so bold,
Tales of the heart, quietly told.

Branches clothed in a frosty guise,
Reflecting the shimmer of dull skies.
Whispers of silence weave through the trees,
A hush that dances upon the breeze.

Every breath hangs, a moment sealed,
In this frozen realm, our fate revealed.
Nature cradles us, soft and warm,
In winter's embrace, we're sheltered from harm.

Frozen echoes linger and play,
Feather-like whispers of the day.
In the quiet, we hear the heart's call,
As snowflakes drift and softly fall.

Amidst this calm, under twilight's glow,
We find the strength in the world we know.
Frozen echoes, secrets unfurled,
Whispering life in a silent world.

Dancing Light on a Blanket of White

A blanket of white covers the ground,
Where joy in silence is easily found.
Softly it sparkles under the sun,
A magical scene where dreams can run.

Dancing light skips over each flake,
Twinkling and glimmering, it starts to wake.
In shadows of whispering trees it plays,
Creating a wonder that never decays.

Each footprint tells stories of hearts entwined,
Warming the chill of days left behind.
With laughter and cheer, we glide and slide,
In winter's embrace, pure joy is our guide.

The world transformed, a stunning sight,
Radiant moments in the soft twilight.
Dancing light weaves through the scene,
Painting our memories, bright and serene.

As day turns to dusk, hues start to blend,
In this tapestry of winter, we mend.
Dancing light on a blanket of white,
In our hearts, it lingers, a pure delight.

The Embrace of Frosty Shadows

Beneath the silvered moonlight's grace,
Whispers linger in icy embrace.
Shadows stretch across the ground,
Silent secrets lost, not found.

Frozen branches gently sway,
Stars above begin to play.
Each breath forms a crystal breath,
In the stillness, we'll dance with death.

Nature's quilt, a blanket bright,
Covers all in purest white.
Frosty fingers touch the air,
In the night, there's magic rare.

Echoes of the twilight's song,
Guide us where we feel we belong.
In the moon's soft, glowing light,
We find solace in the night.

Together in the frosty chill,
Hearts entwine, our dreams fulfill.
In the stillness, love finds ways,
In the frost, our spirits blaze.

Moonlight's Dance with the Sleeping Earth

The moonlight spills on fields so wide,
Casting dreams where shadows bide.
Whispers of the night arise,
Cradled in these serene skies.

Stars twinkle in their celestial waltz,
Nature's pulse, a gentle pulse.
Underneath the silver dome,
The earth lies still, away from home.

Branches cradle in soft light,
Graceful movements of the night.
Each blade of grass bows down low,
In this dance, a quiet glow.

Night creatures stir in soft embrace,
The world slows its frantic race.
Wrapped in calm, a sacred breath,
In the silence, we encounter depth.

Moonlight's grace, forever pure,
In the dark, our hearts endure.
With every step, the night becomes,
A melody with gentle drums.

Over the Cobbled Pathway Lies Whispering Snow

Cobbled stones, a tale in gray,
Cradled whispers of the day.
Underneath the weight of night,
Snowflakes dance in softer light.

Footprints vanish, secrets blend,
The pathway twists, it has no end.
Each step muffled, soft and slow,
In the silence, winds will blow.

Candles flicker in the dark,
Offering warmth, a tiny spark.
Snow blankets all in tranquil glow,
Whispering tales from long ago.

Over the stones, the night does sigh,
As crystals drift from still, cold sky.
We tread lightly, hearts aglow,
Awakening dreams in the snow.

Every flake a story tells,
In the hush, where magic dwells.
Over the pathway, we will roam,
Finding peace, we're almost home.

In the Stillness of a Winter's Dream

In winter's grasp, the world is still,
Frozen landscapes, nature's will.
Echoes soft, drift through the air,
In this silence, we find care.

Blanketed in white and gray,
Time seems lost, slips away.
The moon, a guardian so bright,
Whispers secrets of the night.

Every flake a diamond's dance,
Inviting us into a trance.
With gentle sighs the world breathes low,
In the quiet, dreams will grow.

Branches bow under winter's weight,
Kissed by frost, it feels like fate.
In the stillness, hearts entwine,
In this dream, your hand in mine.

Softly now, let worries cease,
In winter's hold, we find our peace.
Together wrapped in magic's gleam,
In the stillness, we will dream.

Embers of Light in a Sea of White

In the deep night, whispers arise,
Flickers of warmth 'neath endless skies.
Soft glows dance in the chilly air,
Embers ignite, dreams stripped bare.

Beneath the blanket of peaceful snow,
A heartbeat flickers, a gentle glow.
Stars above watch the world below,
Guiding lost souls in winter's flow.

Footprints traced in the silent white,
Stories whispered in the soft twilight.
Moments held in the icy breath,
Voice of life, defying death.

Hope emerges from shadows cast,
Finding light in the darkened past.
Each ember tells of thoughts concealed,
In the night's embrace, hearts revealed.

So let the embers softly gleam,
Weaving truth in a winter dream.
A sea of white, serene and bright,
Carries the warmth of our inner light.

A Stillheart Amidst the Glimmer

In twilight's grace, silence reigns,
Stars awaken, breaking chains.
A still heart beats, deep and slow,
Amidst the glimmer, soft aglow.

Whispers of night kiss the trees,
A gentle breeze brings sweet release.
Lights above and shadows below,
Balance the world in a tender flow.

Memory flickers like candle flame,
In this stillness, nothing's the same.
Time drifts softly, wrapped in lace,
Beneath the stars, we find our place.

In the stillness, we dare to dream,
Follow the glimmer, let spirits scheme.
Hearts entwined in the night so bright,
Together we dance in the soft twilight.

So breathe in deep, let the calm unfold,
Stories await, waiting to be told.
A stillheart gleams, amidst the night,
Hope ignites, a beautiful sight.

Frosted Memories in the Cool Night

Frosted whispers drift through air,
Memories linger, serene and rare.
Each breath taken, a chilly sigh,
Beneath the stars, where echoes lie.

A canvas painted, white and bright,
Trails of shadows in the moonlight.
Frozen laughter floats like mist,
In the cool night, they still exist.

Traces of warmth in the icy blue,
Moments cherished, old yet new.
Stories woven in frost's embrace,
Each glimmer speaks of a time and place.

Embers of joy, as the night unfolds,
Thrill of a secret, softly told.
In winter's blanket, dreams ignite,
Frosted memories, pure delight.

So let us wander, hand in hand,
Through the silence, across the land.
In the cool night, our spirits soar,
Frosted memories forevermore.

Requiem of the Fallen Snow

Softly it falls, a silent woe,
Each flake whispers of things we know.
In the stillness, tales are spun,
A requiem for the day that's done.

Layer by layer, memories heap,
Covering dreams, promising sleep.
Stars weep gently, as night unfolds,
Telling stories that time holds.

Footsteps echo on winter's breath,
A dance with shadows, embraced by death.
But in this stillness, life remains,
Resilience blooms in icy chains.

From depths of loss, blooms a new dawn,
With each new flake, a hope reborn.
Requiem sings through the frozen air,
A promise of spring, whispering care.

So when the snow begins to fade,
Remember each moment, lovingly made.
In the silence, let your heart know,
Life is renewed in the fallen snow.

Flakes like Wishes from the Sky

Softly they fall, like whispers calm,
Each touch a promise, each flake a charm.
Dancing on breezes, in silence they play,
A world transformed in their gentle ballet.

Children's laughter, the magic is clear,
Snowflakes like wishes, they hold so dear.
Building snowmen, with scarves wrapped tight,
Eyes gleam with wonder in the soft twilight.

A blanket of white, so fresh, so pure,
Each flake a story, each moment obscure.
Nature's conclusion, a masterpiece wide,
In winter's embrace, we take joy in the ride.

The ground is a canvas, untouched and bright,
Each flake a dream, igniting the night.
Holding the warmth of our wishes and glee,
Snowflakes like wishes, forever we'll see.

In stillness they settle, with magic they blend,
Creating a world where dreams never end.
So let us remember, as summers pass by,
The joy of those moments, like flakes from the sky.

The Enchantment of a Frozen Evening

The moon casts a glow, so silver and bright,
While shadows unfold in the coolness of night.
Whispers of frost wrap the earth in a trance,
An evening enchanted, a magical dance.

Trees draped in crystals, shimmering light,
Each branch a chandelier, glistening white.
Beneath the stars' gaze, the whispers arise,
Of secrets and dreams spun in midnight skies.

Footsteps are soft on the pristine ice,
Each crunch a reminder of winter's device.
Breath visible, rising, like ghosts in the air,
The enchantment of evening, serene and rare.

Silence envelops, with beauty profound,
In the stillness of frost, a magic is found.
Nature's own lullaby, soothing the day,
As the night drifts onward, and shadows play.

Wrapped in its magic, we linger and gleam,
The night weaves its spell, as we drift into dreams.
A frozen evening, so quiet and clear,
Where warmth fills our hearts as we draw each other near.

Secrets Hidden in the Winter's Glow

Twilight descends, with secrets to share,
Winter's soft blanket curls everywhere.
Amidst the white silence, whispers take flight,
Hidden in shadows, concealed from the light.

Crystals like diamonds adorn every tree,
In the heart of the cold, there's warmth, can't you see?
Stories are woven in each frosty breath,
Life carries on amid shadows of death.

Footprints in snow tell a tale yet untold,
Adventures of children, and memories bold.
Lapdogs and lovers, all wrapped up in light,
Finding their solace on this magical night.

Under the starlight, the world seems to know,
That secrets are waiting, hidden below.
In each little flake rests a wonder untold,
In winter's embrace, our dreams to behold.

So gather around, as the stories unfold,
In winter's warm glow, new memories are gold.
Through laughter and dreams, we will come to discover,
The secrets of winter, each other, our shelter.

A Tapestry of Ice Under Starlight

Twinkling and shimmering, the stars paint the scene,
A tapestry woven of silver and green.
Ice glimmers softly under the deep night,
Crafting a wonderland, breathtaking and bright.

Each breath, a mist in the cold winter air,
Chilling the skin, yet we linger with care.
Nature's own art, each sparkle a thread,
In the fabric of night, where dreams are widespread.

Bare trees reach upward, like fingers they strain,
Tracing the rhythm of frost-laden rain.
This canvas of beauty, as wide as a sigh,
Calls out to wanderers, inviting them nigh.

Gathered in warmth, we share tales of old,
Of starlit adventures, and dreams to unfold.
In this tapestry woven, our hearts intertwine,
Bound by the magic of winter divine.

So let us rejoice in the chill of the night,
Draped in the stars' glow, all hearts feeling light.
In the beauty of ice, we find our way home,
A tapestry of wonder, wherever we roam.